THE SHETLAND PONY

by Gail B. Stewart

Illustrated with photographs
by William Muñoz

Capstone Press

MINNEAPOLIS

Capstone Press • 2440 Fernbrook Lane • Minneapolis, MN 55447

Editorial Director   John Coughlan
Managing Editor   Tom Streissguth
Production Editor   James Stapleton
Book Design   Timothy Halldin

Library of Congress Cataloging-in-Publication Data

Stewart, Gail, 1949-
    The Shetland pony / Gail B. Stewart ; illustrated with photographs by William Muñoz.
        p. cm.
    Includes bibliographical references (p. 44) and index.
    Summary: A brief history and description of the Shetland pony, including its origins in Great Britain and its appeal to children.
    ISBN 1-56065-300-0
    1. Shetland pony--Juvenile literature. [1. Shetland pony. 2. Ponies.] I. Muñoz, William, ill. II. Title.
SF315.2.S5S74   1996
636.1'6--dc20   95-11232
                                                            CIP
                                                            AC

Table of Contents

Quick Facts about Shetland Ponies

Description

Height: American Shetland Ponies average about 42 inches (103 centimeters) tall at the **withers** (the top of the shoulders). But many are smaller, and some are as tall as 46 inches (113 centimeters).

Features: strong hind legs, long head and ears, a very full tail and mane

Colors: black, **bay**, chestnut, **roan,** gray, cream, and **dun**

Development

History: Shetland ponies were used as work horses in the mines of England and Scotland. The first Shetland to come to North America arrived in 1885.

Origin: Shetland Islands of Scotland

Uses

Shetland ponies are used for harness racing, pulling buggies, jumping, and pleasure riding.

Chapter 1

The Best Pony in the World

Some people call it a children's pony. The Shetland pony entertains at the circus and pulls children's wagons at the state fair. The gentle, patient horse allows children to sit on its back and pretend to be cowboys and cowgirls.

Even people who don't know anything about horses have heard of the Shetland pony. Its

The Shetland pony had to be tough to survive the climate and working conditions in its native land.

shaggy coat, long mane, and muscular body make it easy to spot.

Jan Muldoon has been a professional riding instructor for 35 years. According to her, there is no pony that matches up to a Shetland. "I've ridden hundreds of horses. Some were fast Thoroughbreds, others were spirited Arabians. But the horse I remember best is the Shetland pony I had when I was a little girl.

"He was a black pony named Midnight. I began riding him when I was two or three.

Like all horses, Shetland ponies love green pastures and wide open spaces.

Young Shetlands mix with a herd of friendly cows on a western ranch.

When I grew too big for Midnight, it was the saddest time of my childhood. I've never known an animal as smart, as gentle, and as strong. He taught me how to ride."

For many years, people who wanted their young children to learn to ride bought Shetland

ponies. These horses were small and easy to control. Children loved them.

Then things changed. For some reason, parents were in a hurry to get their little ones onto bigger, faster horses, says one horse trainer. They didn't want to get a little pony when their children would just outgrow him in a few years. So they bought an Arabian or a Thoroughbred.

Recently, people have become interested in the Shetland pony again. They are curious about this small and gentle horse. Where did the Shetland come from? Why is it so small? Is it only for children? The answers to these questions are surprising.

A baby Shetland pony works to get steady on its young legs.

Chapter 2

The Shetland Pony's Beginnings

The Shetland pony is known for its gentle nature. But its history is one of struggle, cruelty, and back-breaking work.

"I find myself wondering why Shetland ponies are as nice as they are," admits one man who **breeds** them. "They have had to endure more hardship than any animal ever should."

From the Shetland Islands

Shetland ponies are named for the Shetland Islands, which lie off the northern coast of

Scotland. It is a cold, stormy place. There are no trees, and strong winds and storms batter the islands each day.

Life was difficult on the islands. The people who lived there raised sheep and grew potatoes, turnips, and oats in the rocky soil. Animals had to take care of themselves in the harsh climate. There were no warm shelters, no barns, and little food.

The little Shetland ponies survived by standing patiently while the cold winds blew. They grazed on heather and sour grass. When the grazing was poor, they ate the salty **kelp**, or seaweed, that washed ashore.

Working for a Living

The people of the Shetland Islands needed the pony's help. They used the pony to carry fish home from the docks and heavy baskets of wool to market. Shetland ponies also carried the **peat** that islanders burned to heat their homes.

The Shetland ponies did all these jobs without complaint. "These ponies hauled

The Shetland pony is used to hard work, whether in a damp underground mine or on a snowy prairie.

wagons with loads that horses twice their size would have trouble with," says one historian. "When a farmer was too tired to make the twenty-mile (32-kilometer) walk, he'd sit on the pony's back. The 'Sheltie' was only about 39 inches (1 meter) high, but he'd do that, too!"

Chapter 3

Up From the Mines

Over the years, the people of the Shetland Islands had contact with the mainland of Scotland. People from the mainland heard about these little ponies that worked so hard. Before long, they were coming to the islands to see the Shetland ponies for themselves.

Pit Ponies

These people did not want the ponies for riding or for carrying baskets full of peat. They

A young Shetland nibbles on a pasture. Some of his ancestors worked, ate, and slept underground and never saw the light of day.

The small Shetland pony could handle work in small, narrow spaces.

wanted them as **pit ponies**. This new job would make the ponies' old life on the windy Shetland Islands seem easy.

Pit ponies worked in the underground coal mines of Scotland and England. The little Shetlands could work in the low, narrow mines far more easily than larger horses. They hauled sleds piled with coal from the **coal face**, where the rock was being mined, to tunnels leading to the outside. The tunnels were damp and cold, and the pit ponies suffered greatly.

Clouds of black coal dust hung in the air. The dust clogged the lungs of the ponies and the miners. The miners rarely let the ponies outside to graze. Instead they fed the ponies a few handfuls of grass and a bucket of water.

The work went on day and night. When the workers went home at night, the ponies stayed in the mines. Many of the ponies were born, lived, and died in the mines. They never felt the warmth of the sun.

Goodbye to the Pits

In the mid-19th century, close to 90,000 ponies were working inside the mines. Their suffering ended when inventors created new machines that could do underground work. By the 1930s, there were only 200 pit ponies left.

When the ponies were no longer needed, the miners brought them to the surface. The eyes of the pit ponies were so used to darkness that some were unable to see in the daylight. Their days of darkness and coal dust were over.

The Breeders

Even while many of the Shelties were working as pit ponies, there were some horse breeders in England and Scotland who were interested in them. They thought the small pony would make a good "first horse" for young riders.

When the miners no longer needed the pit ponies, the breeders bought them. They bred the healthiest ponies with other strong Shetlands. They hoped to get young ponies who were as healthy and strong as their parents.

Some breeders in the United States and Canada were interested in the Shetland pony, too. They knew this breed would be as popular with North American children as it already was with English children.

A newborn Shetland pony nestles near its mother.

Chapter 4

The Shetland Pony Up Close

In England and Scotland, breeders have tried to keep the Shetland pony's original features. But in North America, breeders have changed the Shetland pony. They bred it with a taller pony known as a Hackney. As a result, Shetland ponies in the United States and Canada are less boxy and have longer legs than their cousins in England and Scotland.

Measuring Shetland Ponies

Most horses and ponies are measured in **hands**. A hand is a four-inch (10-centimeter) segment. A horse or pony's height is measured from the withers (the spot at the top of the horse's shoulders) to the ground.

Shetland ponies are so small that they are measured in inches, not hands. From the withers to the ground, an English or Scottish Shetland cannot be more than 42 inches (105 centimeters). An American Shetland pony cannot be more than 46 inches (115 centimeters). Shelties can be as short as 36 inches (90 centimeters). Breeders' associations do not allow owners to register ponies that are taller than the allowed height.

The Shetland Pony's Coat

Shetland ponies come in a variety of colors, including black, gray, and bay (a reddish-brown color). Bays have black on their legs, manes, and tails.

Shelties can have color patterns, such as **pinto** and **palomino**. Pinto coloring means that

**To survive the harsh winters of Scotland, the
Shetland developed a thick coat and bushy mane.**

the pony has a mixture of white and another
color. Palomino Shelties are bright gold, with
white manes and tails.

Like their ancestors, modern Shetland
ponies still grow a double-thick coat in cold
weather. When the winds blow, this coat keeps
them warm by trapping the pony's body heat.
When the warm spring sun shines, the pony
sheds the long hairs of its winter coat.

The Shetland pony's tail is as useful as its heavy coat. On windy days, the pony stands with its back to the wind. Its long thick tail fans out, protecting its back legs from the cold air.

Easy to Spot

Those who are familiar with Shetland ponies say that the ponies are easy to spot. "It's not just their size," says one Shetland pony owner.

"The nose is a dead giveaway. Shelties' nostrils are large. This is nature's way of helping cold-weather ponies keep air in their noses longer. That way, frigid air can't hurt their lungs."

Shetland ponies are easily recognized by their small ears, square-shaped heads, and long lips. The long lips help them to unlock stable doors and even open the doors of houses.

"One of my memories as a child has to do with my Shetland pony, Red," says one Shetland owner. "She was the smartest pony on the farm. She loved the smell of warm bread, or pie, or anything my mother was baking.

"Red waited until one evening, when all the loaves of bread were cooling inside the kitchen. She listened as our family walked out the front door to talk to a neighbor. When we came in, Red was standing by the kitchen table, munching on the last loaf of bread. She'd unlatched the back door and just let herself in!"

Chapter 5

The Shetland Pony
in Action

In recent years, horse and pony lovers have rediscovered the Shetland pony. Many parents want their young children to learn to ride. For a time, these parents ignored ponies. Instead, they wanted their children to ride the same breeds that adults ride.

"I think that has changed," says one instructor. "The Shetland pony makes so much

The Shetland pony may be the best horse for beginning riders.

more sense than a Thoroughbred or other type of horse. Kids don't have the same kind of coordination as adults. It takes time to learn balance on a horse or pony. Falling is part of learning to ride, unfortunately. While my daughter is learning, I don't want her falling off a horse that is 14 hands high."

A stable owner agrees. "It makes me nervous to see beginning riders on a big horse. The Shetland is better for beginners than any

other animal. It's gentle, patient, and good-tempered. And when a kid tumbles off, it's a lot shorter distance to fall."

Shetland Pony Events

There are events and competitions for Shetland ponies. These are good opportunities for ponies to show what they can do.

Some of these are riding events. Children aged 14 and under can show off the speed and skill of their ponies. In barrel racing, each team of pony and rider dashes around three barrels set up in a cloverleaf pattern. In these races, balance and agility are as important as speed. Going too fast might result in a barrel being knocked over, and that earns a penalty.

In other events, riders lead their ponies through various tasks. Judges watch carefully as the ponies follow a course that includes fences to jump.

"It's not unusual at all for a Shetland to jump a three-foot (90-centimeter) fence," says one expert. "It's surprising to people who know only that the Shetland is small. They may not know that a Shetland's legs are so strong."

Shetlands in Harness

Other events do not involve riders at all. These are called **harness events**, in which the ponies are harnessed to buggies or carts.

Some adult Shetlands aren't much taller than their offspring.

Harness competitions are not races. Instead, judges watch the pony and driver work together. As the pony pulls the cart around the track, the judges watch to see how well it follows the driver's commands.

There are several **gaits**, or speeds, that Shetland ponies must show at harness competitions. One is called the **park pace**. This is a slow trot, one that a horse and driver might use on a ride around a park.

Another gait is the **smart trot**. This is more difficult, because the pony must raise its legs high in the air. At a smart trot, the legs of the pony must be so high that the front part of the leg is actually horizontal. Some ponies do this naturally, but most must be trained.

To teach the smart trot, many Shetland owners put heavy boots on their ponies. When they take the boots off, its legs seem much lighter to the pony.

Whether a Shetland is used for a child's riding instruction or for fancy harness competitions, people who have worked with the little pony agree that it is a wonderful animal.

A young Shetland pony sits down to take a rest.

A Long Journey

Shetland ponies have come a long way. They have survived the windswept Shetland Islands and the cruelties of the Scottish and English coal mines. Who would have thought that their journey would take them so far?

40

Glossary

bay–a reddish-brown color, with black mane, tail, and legs

breed–to mate certain horses or ponies for the purpose of producing offspring with certain features

coal face–the part of the mountain or rock from which coal is being mined

dun–a grayish brown color

gait–a speed or pace at which a pony or horse moves

hands–four-inch (10-centimeter) segments used to measure the height of a horse or pony

harness event–a competition in which ponies pull their drivers in carts or buggies

The Shetland pony is an easy animal to make friends with. It is gentle, patient, and used to humans.

kelp–seaweed that was often eaten by Shetland ponies

palomino–a color pattern that includes a gold coat, white mane, and white tail

park pace–a slow gait used in harness events

peat–an organic material used for centuries in Scotland and England as fuel for fires

pinto–a color pattern that is a mixture of white and another color, usually black or brown. Many Shetland ponies are pintos.

pit pony–a pony used to drag tubs of coal through the tunnels of a coal mine

roan–a gray-brown, red-brown, or yellow-brown color with small dapples of gray or white

smart trot–a high-stepping gait used in harness events

withers–the top of a pony's shoulders

To Learn More

Chapple, Judy. *Your Horse: A Step-by Step Guide to Horse Ownership*. Pownal, Vt.: Garden Way, 1984.

Griffen, Jeff. *The Pony Book*. Garden City, NY: Doubleday, 1966.

Hess, Lilo. *Shetland Ponies*. New York: Thomas Y. Crowell, 1964.

Henry, Marguerite. *Album of Horses*. New York: Rand McNally, 1951.

Lavine, Sigmund A. and Brigid Casey. *Wonders of Ponies*. New York: Dodd Mead, 1980.

Palmer, Joan. *Know Your Pet Ponies*. New York: Bookwright Press, 1989.

Patent, Dorothy Hinshaw. *A Picture Book of Ponies*. New York: Holiday House, 1983.

Some Useful Addresses

The American Shetland Pony Club
P.O. Box 3415
Peoria, IL 61612-3415

American Humane Association
5351 Roslyn St.
Englewood, CO 80111

American Society for the Prevention of Cruelty to Animals
441 E. 92nd St.
New York, NY 10028

Index